AF487472

LT. WILLIAM L. NEWNAN

ESCAPE IN ITALY

The Narrative of Lieutenant
WILLIAM L. NEWNAN
United States Rangers

ANN ARBOR · UNIVERSITY OF MICHIGAN PRESS · 1945

AN UNCOMMON VALOR REPRINT EDITION
Complete and Unabridged

Printed in the United States of America

ISBN: 979-8-8690-9413-1

TO TED, who, by example, taught his brothers something of courage and an appreciation of values; to all those precious things we take for granted until they are gone, this story, preserved by the energy of thoughtful friends, is dedicated.

Fort Benning, Georgia
March 15, 1945

FOREWORD

THIS IS A BOOK for which there never was an original manuscript. It was recorded in my study as the narrator, without pause or interruption, in simple staccato recitative, told it to his father and mother, a few intimate friends, and me, a day or two after he first returned. The transcript from this recording has been subject to little editing other than that deemed appropriate by the War Department, with the result you are about to enjoy. The original recording is in the hands of the author, and on some far future day his grandchildren may listen to this tale with all its vividness as first told, hearing it in his own vibrant voice as we did, spellbound by the suspense, our imaginations caught by the cool courage, determination, and resourcefulness displayed. On that day, in very truth, none will be able to say that through the years the tale had improved with the telling, and what a tale it will be then, as it is now!

B. E. HUTCHINSON

March 12, 1945

1

WE MET OUR DARK DAY at Cisterna, Italy, on February 1, 1944. Cisterna was a natural point for us to attack for this reason: it was astride the Appian Way, one of the three main roads south to Cassino, and had the Allies controlled the Appian Way to Cassino the Jerries would have been very embarrassed, because it would have been very difficult to bring in food and ammunition, and also reinforcements. That is why the Rangers were pushed into Cisterna.

The plan of attack was as follows. The Rangers were to push for Cisterna, supported on their right by elements from the Third Division. The First Ranger Battalion, followed by the Third Ranger Battalion, was to move along the Mussolini Canal, and the Fourth Ranger Battalion was to act as the support. What happened in Cisterna, in brief, can perhaps best be described in football terms—the old mousetrap play. We had the feeling that we had, perhaps, been allowed to penetrate the lines as a rushing tackle or guard is allowed to penetrate the lines in football and then mousetrapped on either side when we had got through. That was a very dark day for us. The Jerries had a great deal more strength than we thought they had there. As a result, elements of the Third Division, who were to support us by moving up on our right, were stopped entirely and the armored support that was to have come up to us was stopped also. The net result was that we were left pretty much on our own and after a day's fighting, roughly from a quarter of six in the morning until four in the afternoon, we were entirely out of ammunition and the game was finished. (We had left the Anzio beachhead about one o'clock and moved through the German lines during the night.)

Being captured was quite a shock to all of us because we had been able to visualize very graphically the idea of being badly hurt, or perhaps even being killed, but the idea of being taken prisoner was something that none of us had considered at all. As a result we were temporarily off balance.

We were moved immediately on trucks from the Cisterna area to a town about fifteen kilometers away, and put into a large warehouse. We were taken care of at that time very well, I thought, by the Germans. I believe, from talking to other men, that is the usual experience. Front line troops (because they are faced with the same things that you are, and tomorrow may be in the same position you are in) treat you better than rear echelon troops do.

We had the usual questioning all prisoners undergo and our answer was, of course, "All I can tell you is my name, my rank, and my serial number." When we gave that information and refused to give any more the Jerries questioning us would dismiss us. It was rather interesting in that they had two officers acting in the capacity of questioners who spoke perfect English—very fine English. The old stuff was to say, "Of course this is not military information that we are asking you but it will aid us and won't take so long for us and you will save us a lot of trouble, and we would appreciate it." And of course, actually, immediately following that remark would come a question of real military importance. But, as far as I know, our men stuck by their rights—both officers and enlisted men alike—and no information was given.

The next day we were again put on trucks and moved toward Rome and held for a day and a half in an old Interurban roundhouse, well wired and well protected as far as guards and machine guns were concerned. At this point we picked up some British, Canadian, and French Colonial troops. We stayed there about a day and a half and then were put on trucks and moved to Rome. When we had arrived there early in the morning, we were taken to the old Coliseum, then put off the trucks and marched in triumph through the streets of Rome. As we were marching along I was very interested in watching the Italians because I thought, "I will get an indication here of whether they are friendly or hostile, or what their attitude is"—and it was pretty sober and pretty quiet; I could feel that these people were not at all enthusiastic about our being marched through the city. When we had arrived at the other side of the city we were put back on the trucks and moved further north about fifteen miles, to a camp called Fara Sabina.

This camp was typical of a concentration camp or prisoner of war camp; the barracks were enclosed by two double wire fences about ten feet high and about ten yards apart, and between the fences, at the corners, raised about twelve feet above the ground, were guard posts, each guard post facing the back of the one at the other corner. In addition, on each guard post there were searchlights and along the fence, at intervals of twenty-five yards, a pole with a light on it to give further light. On opposite corners from the guardhouses were machine guns and at the other corners the men were armed with rifles and machine pistols. That seems a rather simple arrangement but with it you can handle a very large number of men perfectly safely. Our food was very, very scanty here and had been all along since we left the front line and the jurisdiction of front-line troops. In the morning we received a cup of burned wheat coffee; at noon two Italian wafers—each wafer four inches square and not quite a half inch thick—and a bowl of very thin soup in addition; and in the evening we would again receive a bowl of very thin soup, and no wafers.

At Fara Sabina we did have water to drink, but no water for bathing and no real sanitary facilities. We met some more British officers at Fara Sabina and there I really had a chance to talk with some of them who had been loose for three or four months in the back country. They told me the Italian farmers took very fine care of them; there was plenty of food and they were quite safe as long as they stayed off railroads, roads, and bridges and out of the towns. So I stowed that information away in the back of my mind as a fact that might be useful sometime.

It was here that I met a "pioneer" British officer. By that I mean simply that he had helped to survey the Anzio landing and had been unfortunate enough not to be taken off by the landing craft. He had been back of the lines for some reason, had tried to get through, and had been hit by our own artillery fire on the way and badly wounded. There was no evident wound on the outside, but a piece of the shrapnel had entered his lung and the next day we got him off to the hospital. The Jerries were rather hesitant about moving him, not because of his wound but because they weren't sure he was badly enough hurt to be hospitalized; however we finally prevailed on them.

2

WE WERE ALL LOADED on to trucks and told we were being moved 244 kilometers north; and away we went with one can of what corresponds to our C ration for every two men. The Italian C ration was very small, just a little bit of meat, but it tasted pretty good for it was the first meat we had had. We arrived very late that night at a place called Laterina. Unfortunately, on the way up there we were in covered trucks and it was a fine moonlight night; when it did get dark there was no opportunity of leaping from those trucks. They were fairly well guarded and at the end of the column was a small car loaded with Jerries with machine pistols.

Laterina, as I found later, is located about fifteen kilometers north and west of the Italian town of Arezzo. We arrived late at night and our barracks were in quite a mess. We found just stone floors and no bedding for us the first night; so in our barracks we proceeded to tear up some of the cots and burn them for fires and of course the Jerries were very upset over that. When they wanted us to stop we pointed out that we were supposed to have stoves and bedding and here we were freezing, and the devil with them. They were just confused enough to let us get away with it so we did burn fires all night long.

Our bill of fare was just the same as we had received at Fara Sabina, except that there was no water. That is, the water was contaminated, and if you drank it you did so at your own risk; so your soup ration was also your liquid ration for the day. I had been watching the other men to see whether this thin diet was affecting them; as yet I hadn't noticed much effect, and this was already February 8 or 9. We had been prisoners now for eight or nine days.

I hadn't any idea exactly how I was going to leave this place but we were told that very shortly a Red Cross train was to take all of us north into Germany.

For two reasons I didn't want to go on that trip. For one thing, once in Germany your chances of escaping would be very slim indeed, and secondly, to take that trip was hazardous because our own air force was in complete control of the air, machine gunning and bombing everything that moved.

O'Reilly was my first scout. He was as fine a fighting man as you will find in any army. I was surprised that he did not come to me with some plan of escape before I left Laterina. I heard of O'Reilly later when I was at Oran waiting to come home. Four Ranger non-commissioned officers drifted into Oran; they had escaped north of Florence. Their story really was epic. When the shipment for Germany was ready the enlisted men had been put into box cars and nailed in. The men in two cars, about a hundred altogether, kicked the sides out of their cars and dropped off the moving train. These Rangers certainly raised Cain in the hills around Florence. They naturally had split up into small groups. O'Reilly had obtained a German machine gun from a post which they captured. The last they saw of him, he was leaving to make his way home by himself with the machine gun strapped on his back. He told them he could kill more Germans by himself than in a gang and that he was going to strike off into the hills. They heard later that deep in the hills O'Reilly had found an isolated little town and set himself up there with his machine gun as king of the district. He was literally living the life of Reilly, with everybody deferring to him.

There were about twelve hundred men gathered together by this time and the thing that set me going was the fact that this camp was not in a good state of repair, because it had not many men in it previously, and was falling apart. By that I mean there were no searchlights on the corners, the guard posts had collapsed, and the fences were not as tight and sound as they could be. But the Jerries were fast putting it in shape. They were setting up new searchlights, stringing fresh wire wherever it was needed, and soon this camp would be as tight as Fara Sabina. They were also putting an additional fence around the officers' barracks and I knew that once that fence was up it would be almost impossible to get out of that camp.

In the mornings there was a customary count of the men, and that gave me the idea that in the confusion of that count I might be able to get away from the officer group, get out of our barracks, and begin looking around for a way to get out of the camp. That is exactly what happened. With twelve hundred men to count, and count accurately, it would mean that starting at eight-thirty it would take the Jerries at least until eleven o'clock or quarter to twelve to complete the count. The count the morning I escaped had particular significance; the night before two officers had escaped, and when that was discovered, in the morning of course, the count was much tighter than usual. It was very cold that morning and we would hop first on one foot and then on the other, trying to keep warm. As yet I didn't know just what I was going to do but I saw that I had to do something and do it right away.

When the Germans had finished counting our group they moved us off a little to one side, and since I had no insignia on, this gave me an idea; because our group had been counted, the Jerries were no longer paying a great deal of attention to us. Of course they had found the two officers missing in that count. Right near us was a group of enlisted men standing around and I skipped over and joined them. They were only ten feet away and a very casual movement got me over there, and once over of course I was just lost among the men. Standing there with those men and wondering what to do, I noticed that the group, as closely packed as it was, extended to a building—a long shed close to the fence. For some reason I thought I had better get into that building and just hide, because to date the Germans had only made one count a day and if I got in that building I would have until the check was made again the next morning to figure something out. That was the first step—to get into that building. I kept moving from group to group of enlisted men until I had arrived at the building and then ducked into it rapidly.

In the building were several trucks—I would say five or six—that were being repaired. As I stood there for a little while just wondering what I was going to do, one of our own enlisted men came in, and he could see my tense attitude, and he said, "Lieutenant,"—my collar was open by that time and he could see my insignia—"are you planning to escape?" I said, "I'm thinking about it." He said, "Could I go along with you?" I said, "No, this is only for one man and it may not even work for me. Now get out of here before you bring down some German guards on us." I had no sooner got him out than another one drifted in. I used exactly the same formula on him and had to shoo him out too.

I began to look around the building a little bit and I noticed that one of the trucks was without an engine and it seemed to me that a truck without an engine was a truck that people were not working on. So I went to the truck and opened the cab and climbed in and curled up on the front seat. It was very cold. My teeth were chattering. I had my pocket watch and I said, "Now you just lie here without moving until quarter of twelve; you won't move until quarter of twelve and the fact that you are so terribly uncomfortable here probably means that you are doing just the right thing"

I hadn't been in the truck more than fifteen minutes when some Italian mechanics, Fascists in German pay who were working on the trucks, came in. They proceeded to work on the trucks and of course their presence in there meant to the German guards outside the building that no one was in that building. It got colder and colder in that truck, and I kept lying there, and it seemed years, but finally quarter of twelve did roll around. I slipped out of the truck.

3

T HE MECHANICS HAD LEFT for lunch at eleven-thirty. By keeping down low, I could not be seen through the windows by the guards outside. There was a door that opened on the side where the fence was. I went through the door and sat down with my back against the building. The fence was then only about ten feet away and the wings of the building extending out to my left and right just hid me from the guards who were on the inside of the stockade. They were there to herd the prisoners, as you would herd a large bunch of sheep or cattle.

There were Jerries moving around on various duties outside the fence, but they would look in and see me sitting there calmly in the sun with my back to the building and were sure of course that the guards inside knew I was there and that it was all right. In other words, it was simply a case of confusion—one person thinking that the other person knew something that he did not. I had counted, as I lay in that truck and had tried to develop some logical plan, on three things, and I had already put one into execution. In a morning count of twelve hundred men—our ranks had by that time been swelled to that number by elements of the Irish Guards, the Forty-fifth Division, the Third Division, and some miscellaneous British officers—there had been a good deal of confusion.

Secondly, guards, like most men, are not apt to be as alert in the daytime as at night. They are frightened a little bit and they are afraid that there might be something in the shadows; at night they are alert and in the daytime they relax. Third, everyone's mind was pretty well concentrated on food at noontime. (Our diet was slim but the diet of the German guards was also slim. They were not receiving very much more to eat than we were.) I counted on those three things and they were working fairly well so far.

Then I almost fell into my own trap. I heard the mess kits rattling for lunch and I could smell the food from the mess hall and I got so hungry that I said, "You'd better call this a day and go and get your food and think about escaping some other time." And then, fortunately, looking at the outside fence, the outer of the two fences, I noticed there was a jagged hole that had not yet been repaired, large enough to let a man through, bending over. I made up my mind that I was going. A couple of strides brought me to the inner fence. I had selected a good strong-looking pole to climb and was over in no time and dropped in between the two fences and ducked through the hole in the outside fence. Of course, by the time I was through the hole in the outside fence I was far enough away from the building so that the wings no longer protected me from the vision of the guards. In fact, when I was on top of the first fence, they could have seen me had they turned around. But they didn't turn around.

Now straight ahead of me, about twenty-five to thirty yards, was a group of buildings. I had selected a time when there were no Jerries on the outside of the fence; at least I couldn't see any of them. They had gone into mess and the first job was to get those buildings in between me and the guards in the enclosure so they couldn't shoot. I had a hard time stopping myself from running at that point, but I figured that if I was walking casually, but rapidly, even if the guards did turn around they would not know why I was out there. I wouldn't be running, so obviously I wouldn't be escaping; and in any event it would confuse them enough so they might not shoot. But they didn't turn around. I was never faced with that problem.

I had just rounded one of the buildings and got it in between me and the guards when the Italian mechanics that had been eating lunch in that building suddenly walked out. They didn't know what to make of me walking along there; so they called the master mechanic, who came out. He didn't know what to make of me, either, so he began to jabber at me. That was my cue that this walking business was over, and so I bolted on a dead run. Then the Italian master mechanic began to yell and shout and wave his arms; but that meant nothing to the Germans inside the enclosure, because everything was peaceful in there. They couldn't see him; all they could do was hear him; and as only one German in a thousand really understands Italian, they didn't know what he was yelling about.

There was another fence two hundred yards outside the main stockade, and in the old days they would have had a guard out there; but since they were short handed they didn't, and that was a lucky thing for me. Of course I was over that fence in nothing flat and then just kept running as fast as I could go. Now I hadn't seen the ground out there; this whole process was just one step to the next step. It wasn't well thought out in advance; there was no way of thinking it well out in advance. But on my immediate left was the River Arno. That is, I was near the source of the River Arno—the south spur—and from there it travels on, swings north and then swings west and forms the natural barrier, on which the Gothic Line is now, and empties into the sea around Pisa. Three or four hundred yards to my right was a highway; so I was caught between those two, and it meant that if I wasn't going to get caught, I had to get out of that. I couldn't simply run right straight ahead. The main thing to do then was to cross this river immediately. Either I would have to swim it, or I would have to ford it.

As I ran along the bank I noticed that the water was breaking white in the river about a hundred yards ahead of me. That meant it must be shallow there—a ford. I went in and it was just about knee deep but very swift and about sixty yards wide. The last four or five feet before I could reach a little bar projecting out from the bank was tough. I was afraid I was going to be swamped, but an Italian farmer working in his fields with his big white oxen saw me and my difficulty, for I was going very slowly across the river; in fact, it seemed as if I was just creeping, and of course I was worrying about the Jerry guards that would soon be after me. He held his fork out to me and I grabbed hold and he pulled me up. He didn't say anything and I didn't say anything; we just understood each other.

And then I took off on a run again, now making for the high ground. Not only making for high ground, but doubling right back on the camp and still keeping the river between me and the camp. I had just reached the high ground about four or five hundred yards from the river and had lain down in some cover when along the bank, trotting from the way I had come, came six Germans, looking for me. They had finally found out what was going on but they couldn't see anything. The Italian across the river didn't tip them off, and they couldn't leave twelve hundred men at the camp with inadequate guards to look for one man; so they had to turn around and go back. That was my cue that I could again start moving with relative safety.

4

I DIDN'T KNOW FOR SURE which direction was which, for at that time of year (this was February 8 or 9) the sun doesn't rise due east and travel directly across your head and set due west. It rises somewhere in the east and swings across your front to the south and sets somewhere in the west, but that isn't good enough to travel by. So I just kept blundering along. The first job was to get rid of my uniform or to get something that would cover it up. I hadn't gone more than three-quarters of a mile from camp, traveling over very wet and rolling ground, with no roads—a good factor—when I saw three Italian farmers, apparently either relatives or brothers, working in the fields. I had to hazard everything, so I decided that I was going to take my chance right then. I walked up to these men; of course I couldn't speak Italian and they couldn't speak English, but they could tell the whole story simply by looking at me.

After standing there for about two or three minutes while both the Italians and I tried to use sign language, they threw their bags over their shoulders and motioned me to go with them. I did. From there, we went, I would say, about a half-mile, still over fields and with no roads anywhere except little dirt trails. When we had got quite near one farmhouse, the other two went on. The one chap led me up to the house, and then went back to the fields and left me. The women and all the children and the dogs rushed out, and the chickens cackled and everything was there to welcome me. They could tell by my uniform immediately that I was either an Englishman or American. Their big term was *Inglese;* they thought perhaps I was an Englishman. So they immediately got out their *vino* and a big loaf of bread, and of course I was mighty darn hungry; so I tore right into it. Not having had anything to eat for quite a little while, and not having had anything to drink for a long while, particularly with alcohol in it, I had no more than got down about three-quarters of this bottle than I was all ready to go back and take the prison camp apart. Fortunately I restrained myself, but I was really fit to fight the world at that point. We sat there gesturing to each other. They saw that my feet were wet, and insisted on getting me a pair of socks, and dragged out an old pair of trousers, an old mackinaw, an old hat, and a scarf. I sat there until evening, eating and drinking and wondering if the Jerry patrol was really going to wise up and start to comb the country.

Then the man of the house came back. The Italian farmer knocks off about three-thirty and comes in and putters around, straightening his barn up and feeding his cattle like any farmer, but a little earlier than our men do. And about six o'clock he is all done work and eats a very light meal for the evening. I had on a very good combat jacket and I could see the Italian admiring it. I couldn't very well take it with me and when he offered to put me up for the night I immediately said, "Well, now I want you"—this was all in gestures of course—"to have this jacket in exchange for these clothes you have given me." That tickled him to death. He took the jacket and put it away. I started to go out to sleep in the haystack that night, but they missed me and came out and dragged me out of the haystack and put me up in one of their best beds, which was a terribly hazardous thing for them. In other words, I could have been just as lousy as could be and you can imagine what would have happened to that bed shortly. But they were really hospitable souls.

I stayed there two days and three nights. While I was there one of the boys, or rather the boy of one of the other chaps, who was considered the student of the neighborhood, was called over with his little atlas. He didn't have a really good map of Italy but he did have a school kid's map which had all of Italy on about six inches, and it had some of the towns on it, and they pointed out that I was near Arezzo. Of course I knew immediately about where I was; that is, about 240 kilometers due north of Rome, because when the Germans moved us from Fara Sabina they told us they were taking us on a trip of 244 kilometers.

So I had a few facts now and I had the map, and then I decided to take off and get somewhere. They insisted on giving me a bottle of *vino* and a loaf of bread, which I carried in a little satchel, and off I went. I had the scarf around my neck covering my uniform so that you couldn't see my shirt, and an old slouch hat, the mackinaw buttoned up, and the borrowed trousers on, so that from a distance I could be just an Italian farmer walking along.

5

I TRIED TO GO BY A SENSE of direction and thought I was going south, but after traveling three-quarters of a day and inquiring at a farm house and using the same method that I had used on the first farmers—asking about Rome and pointing where I thought south was—I found out that what *I* thought was south *they* said was north. I wouldn't believe 'em until they dragged out the few maps they had, and finally by pointing to a mountain and learning what its name was, I decided that was north after all.

At that house they said I must come with them, that there was an escaped prisoner in another house; so I was taken over there and not long after I got there a Frenchman was brought to me who spoke very little English but spoke Italian fluently. The war was over for him; he had been one of the French soldiers garrisoned in Algeria that had been taken earlier in the war and he was just going to settle down and become an Italian. He was this farmer's right-hand man. I stayed there one night and they told me that farther on down the line I would find an English captain. The Frenchman was going to lead me there. The next morning, bright and early, we started off. When we got to the house the farmer was very suspicious, but I produced my AGO card, that is, the officer's identification card, which the Germans had not taken from me, and I finally convinced him that I was all right. I was taken out in the field near the house and introduced to an English chap (an enlisted man) along with a bunch of Italian youngsters—five or six who were just of draft age and were hiding to avoid the German labor draft. I stayed at that place one night. I tried to get the English chap to go along with me, but he had been holed up there for six months and he was going to wait for the lines to pass over him. He would rather stay right there as he had a pretty good billet.

While I was there I met an Italian who was learning to speak English and was very proud of what he knew and not a bad sort of person at all. He insisted on helping me along all the time and finally, to make use of this chap, who was beginning to bother me a little bit, I had him write out a brief dictionary of the words I thought I would need most going south. He wrote down about fifteen or twenty of these on a piece of paper. Those, in addition to what I picked up, were the Italian words I traveled on the rest of the time.

I remembered my former experience of just blundering around because of trying to guess at directions by the sun, and walking along valleys and getting all mixed up; so I recalled that the Army had taught us in school how to use a pocket watch as a compass. I had a pocket watch that hadn't been taken away, which I could use very easily in this manner; point the hour hand at the sun and then bisect the angle—the smaller of the two angles between the hour hand and twelve o'clock—and get due south. It won't give absolutely due south unless the watch is on sun time (or let's say, set by an almanac as to when the sun rises) but a watch is generally close enough anyhow, and mine was. I could set a south line in that way. I took a peak way off that corresponded with that line and then walked toward that peak in an absolutely straight line over anything in the way. Using my watch as my first sight I set off from this place, and just kept going.

It was very rough country. It isn't what we would call mountains but they are really rugged hills and that time of year it was wet and damp, hard going, not over roads, of course, but over plowed fields and up and down mountains. It was so hard that I would keep saying to myself— and I still think it was right—"The hard way is the best way, for if it is such hard going for you in here, the Jerries certainly aren't going to be back in here for fun, and they will have to know you are here before they will ever start to come in to get you. You are not just going to blunder into something that you shouldn't blunder into."

I began to perfect a system that I used all the way down. The farmers, as I said before, quit work about three-thirty; so about three-thirty I would begin to look around for a good looking farmhouse and about that time of day the farmer would just be coming in with his oxen and begin to cut hay out of the rack. Then with my schoolkid's map and a later map that I had picked up, which was a little more detailed, in my hand, I would walk up to him, well knowing where Rome was, and ask him if Rome were in that direction, and I would point south. That would start the conversation. Of course he wouldn't have to look at me twice, and see my good shoes, army shoes, before he knew all about my being an escaped prisoner. Then the question was what kind of prisoner was I—British or American? Pretty soon either he would invite me down to his house or I would invite myself, and then I would produce all my documents and would cause quite a sensation in the house. Naturally these people were cut off from the world, with no amusements. Then the first thing they knew it was getting dark outside, and they had to invite me to stay the night. While they did get up early in the morning, they never had anything to eat at all until around eight-thirty, and I didn't want to leave without any food. That meant the day of travel was from approximately eight-thirty until four o'clock in the afternoon. I traveled only during daylight as the country was too rugged to knock around in at night.

I had talked to the British prisoners and they told me that the old battle line was a very hard one to get through. Thinking it over, I decided the best bet was to make right for Rome, as I was convinced that the Anzio beachhead would be extended shortly. The whole question simply resolved itself into reaching the outskirts of Rome just prior to the time that our boys arrived there and then holing up somewhere and letting the line pass over me. That would be the easiest way; and so I headed straight south for Rome.

I didn't have any trouble except one time, and then I came just about as close to being picked up as I ever want to. I was attempting to avoid the airfield at Chiusi; or rather I thought there was an airfield there. The reason I thought so was that I had had to come down out of the mountains finally, down into the plain by the Arno River, at the point where the Tiber is visible. I really felt unprotected getting out of my mountains and I know why Kipling wrote "Hillmen desire their hills," because when you are in the mountains you are safe. When you are down on the plain you are surrounded on all sides by enemies, or you feel you are.

I could see the bridge crossing the Tiber where the Arno and the Tiber nearly join and I knew that would be a place where plenty of Jerries were guarding, so I began to flank it to the west. I was flanking to the west because as I came down due south I was already west of the Arno and Tiber Rivers and to flank anything to the east would have meant re-crossing the river. I made a slight error there because Orvieto or Chiusi, I don't know which it is, was guarded by an airfield at Allerona, and Allerona on my map looked as if it was much farther back, much farther to the west than it was. So I flanked right smack into Allerona; not into the town itself, but right into the airfield protecting it.

There was no going back because I had climbed a very steep escarpment and had walked a good two or three hundred yards when I suddenly saw what had happened to me and I simply couldn't turn around. I just kept going ahead and the first thing I knew I was walking over some freshly dug gun emplacements, apparently alternate positions, so that the defenses could be shifted in case of bombings. About the time I got by those emplacements I heard voices and ducked down and there came a Jerry patrol going to work. I proceeded a little further, into a cemetery, sat down for a little to collect my wits, looked out, and saw that I was on a bluff that a road was cut through. I was practically at the main gates of Allerona and along the road were Jerry wiring parties, Italian mechanics, and Italian labor gangs. Across the road was a vineyard. My problem then (and I was scared stiff, and didn't know what the devil to do) was to get across the road and into that vineyard for some sort of safety, and then worry about what I was going to do next.

There was nothing to do but go right ahead, so I slipped down the bank, though I didn't like that at all. There was no easy way. I had to drop down a ten-foot bank; a rather strange way for a strange man to appear on a road, by skidding down a bank. I figured that was a danger point, but there was nothing else to do. Of course I felt horribly conspicuous. I was constantly being referred to as a big man. Actually I was the smallest of all the Ranger officers, but in this part of Italy, and even in the north country where men are much bigger, I was considered a large man. Very few Italians were as tall as I. In addition to that, I was wearing my glasses, and in the country they just don't wear glasses. If their eyes are bad that it just too bad; it is God's curse on them. They don't have any glasses. A man wearing glasses and of my height, with good army shoes, although they were covered with mud, was, to my mind, a perfect character to suspect.

I got across the road all right, and there was a little gate into the vineyard. I opened the gate and slipped through, then pretended to be busy working on the vines; but of course people don't do much work on vines that time of year unless they have a pair of clippers in their hands and are clipping and cutting them back. While I was standing there I pulled my pipe out to get nonchalant with it; I had bought the pipe, with a little sack of tobacco, from one of the German guards just outside of Rome for a dollar and a half. I was just getting ready to go across to a little brick house, when, lo and behold! the door opened and ten Jerries walked out of that house. They came right down the path about fifty yards away, paid absolutely no attention to me, and went on to work.

As soon as they were gone I said, "I won't take that path; I will take this one to the right." I took the path to the right, which was going up on to high ground. The path went up to the right and then down into the valley, which the Jerries had just come across, and then up again. I was struggling along up this path nearly to the top, when I saw a fence ahead of me. There was no use stopping then, so I kept on, getting rather fatalistic by that time. I was badly enough shocked the first ten minutes to be no longer capable of being shocked; and inside the fence, when I got up to where I could see, was a Jerry sentry walking around a gun emplacement. A bunch of men were sleeping in there on shift. The sentry didn't even stop in his stride—just looked at me, and I looked furtively at him and kept walking.

To the right, on a little bit higher ground, was a quarry where they had been digging stone. I walked on across a flat field and just before I got out of the weeds, which were about head high, I saw another emplacement ahead of me, and suddenly I began to think. "You are doing something terribly wrong to be running into all these emplacements. Even if you are around an airfield you shouldn't run into emplacements so much." I sat down and tried to light my pipe again to think over what the devil was wrong, or if there was anything wrong, or if I was just in a jam, and then I thought, "Well, you *are* stupid." Because coming down the whole trick had been always to stay on high ground for two reasons: first, you could always see from high ground and you could go down either the right slope or the left slope if you were chased, and, second, you didn't have to walk up and down hill that way; you were walking along ridge lines and didn't wear yourself out. But there I was near an airfield, and, naturally, anti-aircraft guns are placed on high points. In following my old method of instinctively seeking high ground, I was getting myself into trouble.

I immediately looked around to see how I could get off this high ground. I didn't want to backtrack. There was about a fifty- or sixty-foot drop down into a valley but a good crevice led down. Of course farmers don't climb up and down crevices, that was bad; I didn't want anyone to see me working my way down the crevice; but there was nothing to do but to go down. I did. Almost always I would find that although that country did not have roads, it was just full of little paths. There was a path along the valley floor and I followed it, keeping right to the valley all the time, and gradually it began to rise and took me out beyond these gun emplacements, about a mile and a half beyond, into a little Italian town.

It was the one and only Italian town I ever walked through on my way down, and I had to because the path led right in, and I just took the gamble. I noticed everyone turning and looking at me; I wasn't fooling any Italian. They didn't know who I was, but they did know I wasn't a native. I was protected there too, in a way, because the country was full of men streaming home—Italians from the north who had been put into German labor battalions. They had got sick and tired and had started home. So people didn't pay much attention to traveling men. There were men moving all the time all over the country. They didn't know who I was but I didn't look right to them. I got out of there in a hurry and kept going south.

I would keep checking on these towns with my map to make sure my watch compass was working (and it was, perfectly). I had a double check because every so often I would come to high ground, and far to my left, or far to the east, I could see the railway going down to Rome. After I had got by Montefiascone I could see, way ahead of me, a mountain. The country had now flattened out considerably, and I later found that this mountain is one of the few single mountains in Italy—that is, mountains that just stand in a plain without any other mountains around them, and is a natural point for anybody moving from north to south to use as a guide.*

---

* This is Mount Soratte, the ancient Soracte celebrated by Horace (*Odes* i.9), Vergil, and others, a fragment of a former chain of the Appennines which was overwhelmed by the volcanic upheaval of this region. It is crowned by the Monastery of San Silvestro, founded in 746 by Carloman, son of Charles Martel and brother of Pepin the Short.

6

As I GOT CLOSER AND CLOSER to Rome, the hospitality was getting poorer and poorer and the country poorer and poorer and there were more roads. I discovered that the hospitality offered by the people in the country varied exactly with their proximity to a good road. In other words, good roads meant Jerries, and if there were Jerries near or Jerries that could be brought in the Italians wouldn't do much for you. They had too much at stake themselves. However, if there weren't roads, they were in their own little castles and very independent, and I had played up to that by telling them, in my horrible Italian, a statement something as follows. I would say to them, *"Il vado Roma departe presto demane mattina,"* all of which was supposed to mean that I was going to Rome and would leave very rapidly in the morning; and since news takes longer than a few hours to filter out, they figured they could risk that one day. I never did stay, after I started to move, over one day.

I kept bearing down on Rome, and I began to think that I was as bad as the Italian immigrants that go to America and think of New York as the Golden City. I did have an occasional check with the radio; I would find some family that had one, and then I would hear the talk and I would think, "You are kind of silly, for there is nothing worse than a big city without friends or money. You are much better in the country." I had just about made up my mind that I wasn't going to Rome. The question was just where I was going—whether I would stop on the outskirts of Rome and wait, or try to get through the lines.

I crossed the main highway to Rome, still using the mountain as a guide. If you guide on that mountain you cannot help but run into the grotto where two British chaps, Chicken and Dinger, off the British submarine *Saracen,* live. On these submarines they give everybody a nickname. Dinger, for instance, was Bell in real life and Chicken—I forget his name, but he was a little fellow and they weren't going to dignify him with the name Rooster, so they decided to call him Chicken. They were living, and had been living, in this grotto along the stream, for six months. A grotto is any kind of protection from the weather. In this case it was simply a half cave in the rock with a good fissure along one side to let the smoke out when you built a fire in the corner of the cave. I hadn't any more than crossed the road when it started to rain, and I began looking for cover.

Of course the country was pretty full of Jerries now, as I was getting into their area, but I still had to take a chance; so I walked up to a farmhouse and took the usual chance with the usual success. They took me in and fed me, and right away they told me about the two British fellows and said, "We are going to take you to them." So I said, "Fine!" They took me about a half-mile out to a stream, a very rough and wild little stream with the banks very thick and heavy with vegetation, and took me down to a little shack where a fellow named Franco lived. With Franco another fellow was sitting. Before he said a word to me he spiels a lot of Italian lingo back and forth to Franco. I don't know who he is, but after he has figured out that I am all right he tells me, "I am British." That was my introduction to Chicken, who took me along with him to the grotto.

Just before I came down, two Americans had come in from Orte, which is about forty or fifty miles from Civitavecchia—that was this town. Now it is not the coast town of Civitavecchia, that was so badly bombed; it is an inland town by the same name. These chaps, in their stories, confirmed any fears that I had had about traveling to Germany on a train. There were five hundred of them loaded on a train. The Jerries didn't have sufficient guards, so they had nailed the boys into the box cars to keep them from jumping out. The train had been moving along near Orte when our bombers had come over, probably not after the train at all, but after the bridge that was near by. The engineer had funked it badly and deserted his train right on the bridge. The bombers came over to their rendezvous and dropped their load. The first flight of bombs tore the ventilator off the car these two boys were in and they were able to get out. But the sight hadn't been accurate on that first run and the bombers turned and made a second run. Their second run was a dead hit on the bridge, and out of those five hundred men on that train about two hundred and fifty to three hundred were either blown to pieces or knocked off into the water and drowned. That was a pretty graphic illustration of what can happen on a long train-ride to Germany when the Allies are controlling the air.

These two chaps didn't encourage me as to the Rome situation. They had tried to go on to Rome and had found the hospitality too poor and the country too darn barren. They had turned around and come back, and these English fellows very graciously had taken them in. That meant that this poor chap Franco, their *padrone,* who had been supporting them for six months, now had two more to support. His faith was magnificent. He had been doing all this simply on a chit promising to pay.

In fact, I had found those chits all over the country on the way down. No sooner had the farmers decided that I was all right than they would pull out a chit to show me. The chit read something like this: "This is to certify that these people have given me food and shelter for two days. (Signed) Corporal Mahoney, Co. D, ... outfit." And then dated. The country was just flooded with them. What had happened was that the Italian prison camps were thrown open last year by the September armistice and all these fellows flooded out onto the country. There were thousands of them.

Because of conflict in orders, many chaps would often sit around camps and three or four days later along would come a Jerry and close the camps up again; and hardly any of them I found had moved very far from camp. In other words, they were waiting for the lines to come to them, so I would find them not very far from their camps. Chicken and Dinger were excellent illustrations, because their camp wasn't over twenty-five miles to the west of this town. It was a camp where they took submarine men to question.

All the way down these Italians would promise you all sorts of things when they were in the protection of their homes and under the influence of two or three glasses of *vino* and talking about killing *tedeschi*—that is, killing Germans. They would say, "I will bring you some cigarettes today or tomorrow," and tomorrow would come and they never did bring them or never thought about the cigarettes. It was just a nice thing to say, but not to do. So when I got here, pretty soon some Italians that were friendly came along and Chicken and Dinger said, "These guys are bad guys; they promised to get us some money here and we think they did, but they stole it. They took our name, rank, and serial number to the Vatican to get money, and theoretically that is to be returned to us; but we just never got it."

When these Italians arrived I was going to find out what the score was. I gave them my name, my rank, and my serial number, although Chicken and Dinger kept insisting that I give them a phoney name, rank, and serial number so they couldn't fleece us. But in any event I gave them the correct facts because they promised to see that that name was transmitted home. Even if these men were so unreliable as to make money out of the deal, they would have to get that name to responsible people, and the name would, of course, then be transmitted home. That was the set-up.

They told us about a saboteur gang that was supposed to be operat-

ing in the neighborhood, run by a chap called "the Prince" who claimed
to be of nobility—Italian nobility. I thought this an excellent time to
see if there was anything in all this talk, so I told these fellows I would
be delighted to blow any bridge, to shoot any Germans, just as long as
they furnished the dynamite and came along. They said the Prince
would be along in five days.

I stayed with Chicken and Dinger for five days and then a rather
amusing thing happened. It sounds amusing now but it wasn't then.
One of these American boys, a chap called Winter, was literally lousy
when he came in, but he didn't tell anybody. It was pretty cold at night
and we would try to keep a fire burning, but it was still cold. They had
thrown some straw on the floor of this cave. They were four, and I made
five. The blanket was just long enough to cover four. As I had the
heaviest clothing, I slept in one corner and of course Winter lay right
down snugly in the middle, lousy as could be. You can imagine how
nice and warm it was in the middle, and pretty soon, about two days
after I got there, these fellows began to scratch and look around, and
they were covered.

In the country this is no joke, because the Italians only have about
one set of clothing after being through about six or seven years of war.
It meant that you had to boil everything. I was laughing; I had been
sleeping in the cold and they hadn't bothered to come to me because
they don't travel much; they stay where it's warm.

The other four fellows had to take all their clothes off and throw
what homemade tobacco we had into the water to make it a strong solu-
tion, which incidentally dyed everything. They piled all their clothes in
the tank. They were shivering around in their birthday suits. They
didn't have anything to put on. They tried to wrap up in the blankets
but even the blankets had to be thoroughly shaken and aired so they
really didn't have a blanket when you got right down to it. There they
were, all dancing around. Finally, they got their stuff, and of course
after the stuff was boiled it took all day to dry out; but they finally did
get it back on.

Then, as I expected, at the end of five days no Prince arrived. These
Italians were very volatile. Near us was an airfield and every so often
the Allies would come over and bomb it. When they bombed it the
Italians couldn't do too much for us; but it only took 'em two days to
forget us, and two days later we would have to go out and beg for bread.

Two Italians were supposed to be underground and they kept telling us about the radio transmitter they had. They knew the Americans were going to bomb the airfield every so often and they said, "Now we have transmitted just where this airfield is," and next day, of course, it just happened to be the next day, over came the Americans and bombed the field. They came running back to us, all smiles, and said, "See, our message got through." Of course there was no transmitter anywhere around and none of them knew how to operate it anyhow. In fact, they had asked me if I knew how to operate one.

Since no Prince came and the place seemed to be getting dangerous, I decided to pull out. I don't know what happened to my friends, because Winter was quite a drinker, they had a little money, and Dinger was getting fed up and was beginning to drink. And the same little wine shop in a grotto (having been bombed out of town) that they went to was a wine shop that the Jerries from the airfield patronized. Sometimes these fellows would be up there when the Jerries were there, and they would just sit and keep quiet and drink their wine. When Dinger was up there, speaking perfect Italian, he would join in the conversation and talk to all of them. But it was getting a little bit too doggoned risky, as everyone in the neighborhood knew we were there and everybody knew just who we were. With the failure of the Prince to show up, and for other reasons, I decided to push on. Because our sanitary conditions were bad, I had had a touch of diarrhea, and it was time to get out of there before I got really sick. So I kept moving.

7

THAT COUNTRY IS FLAT, but it is strange country in that it is just covered with washes and deep gashes. By that I mean washes that are maybe a hundred feet deep and three or four hundred feet wide; they just seem to be there for no reason at all. They go for three or four miles and then gently slope up at the end and right back into the rest of the country. You can't afford to walk along the ends and keep to the road; you've just got to cross 'em. It started to rain toward the end of the day and I was pretty well tuckered, having crossed three or four. They seemed endless and all of them were diabolically at right angles to my course. It wasn't any question of walking along the bottom of one; you had to cross every one of them.

It was beginning to rain and I was plugging along when ahead of me I saw a very ragged-looking Italian in an old tattered uniform. I wanted to ask him what the situation was in the house ahead. I stopped him and in my horrible Italian began to ask him about the Germans. After one look at his blue eyes and square-cut face and hearing him talk with a pronounced British accent, I knew just whom I was talking to, another escaped prisoner and another man off the submarine *Saracen*. He thought I was a German. I told him I was an American and began to talk it, and then he knew I must be. So I said, "Let's get out of this rain," and he took me to his grotto.

Everything that shelters you is a grotto. But this grotto was a super-de luxe one. It was an old Roman burial vault very neatly hidden in the hills. Of course it had about a foot of water in all but one corner, but it did have a roof over it and you could build a fire, and he had two beds built in there just off the floor.

By this time I had decided that Rome was definitely out, and as I walked along that day I had decided the thing to do was to try and hit through the lines at Sulmona. To do that I wanted a good man with me, one that I could absolutely count on, because in the mountains, if you fall down and break a leg or an ankle or something, you want someone to pull you out and get you to a place where you can get some help. This looked like just my man. Of course I didn't know whether he would want to come, but his condition looked wretched to me, even after what I had been living through (which hadn't been bad because I had been pretty lucky). This poor chap, living in the grotto with very little food, seemed in a bad way, and I thought it was time to broach the subject. But first I heard his sad story; then I knew I had my man.

A group of them off the submarine *Saracen* had been living in a little town in houses right inside the town itself, even though a German garrison of a few men was in town too—maybe fifteen or twenty Germans. They had become quite confident and cocky and were working in the arbors along with the Italians, and moving about fairly freely in the evenings. There were a couple of South Africans who at the winery got a little bit high and felt the old Nordic blood beginning to surge back and forth in their veins under the influence of the *vino*. So they walked up to two Germans and slapped them on the back and told them that after all they were good scouts and the same blood and all the rest of it. The Jerries bought them a few more drinks and said, "Why, your shoes are in deplorable shape and after all we are blood brothers; you come along with us and we'll take you down and get some shoes," and of course as soon as they got them outside they pulled their pistols on 'em and marched right down to the commandant.

These two chaps spilled the beans; where the prisoners were, who was taking care of them, and everything. There was a roundup and Bennett got away only by leaping out of a second story window. His *padrone* (that is the word for any one that takes care of you) was a woman whose husband was missing in Albania, and she had been very kind to this chap even after this happened. Even knowing that her house was being watched, she had continued to carry him food twice a week, about three kilometers out of town, and leave it for him. But she had got mixed up one day and hadn't brought his food; so when I arrived Bennett had just received his ration, after a whole week without anything except the scraps left from the last one. When I began to talk to him about how well I was faring, as long as I didn't exhaust hospitality by staying over one day, he said that he would like to come along. The next day we started out together, carrying what little food was left.

Our plan was this. The mountain was a son-of-a-gun to get around. It looked small, but you had to keep walking and walking and walking, and it would still stay right on your flank all the time. I had decided to go through Sulmona. To go through at Sulmona meant you had to start at the southeast and recross the Tiber River; to do that you had to get around the mountain which I had guided on. Not only that, we had to get well around it because we were told there was a German garrison right at its base—the south base of the mountain. Finally we thought we were far enough south and started cutting east. Again we had these gullies which should have been parallel with our course, but again they were at right angles, and we crawled up and down those things all day long. We had a big thrill when we crossed the main highway to Rome; we felt like desperate conspirators going over this road. Of course, actually, nobody was paying a darn bit of attention and unless we had walked right into a Jerry we were perfectly okay. Although Bennett looked like a scarecrow in his clothes and I looked almost as bad, we got safely across and kept well away from roads and ordinary houses.

I was beginning to pride myself on my ability to pick a good billet for the night; so after a while, when it began to be around four-thirty, I said, "There is a good house; there is where we are going to be taken care of." We walked right up, and Bennett began talking in his horrible Italian and I took my watch out and tried to fix our directions. A phono-

graph was playing somewhere in the house, and two women dashed out
and rushed us around and put us in the stable. Three Jerries were in
the house, who came out every week-end to have a little *vino* and dance
with the girls and get a little country food. So there we were; we could
have been picked up just as easy as duck soup. They left us in the
stable, and pretty soon the Germans went away, and they invited us in
and gave us *vino* and cigarettes. They were pretty well stocked, for the
Germans were trading their food for the food that these people could
give them. But it was too hot there and they moved us about five hundred yards to some goat herders—just a little thatched hut, but they took
very good care of us.

We hadn't been there very long, only a couple of hours (it was only
about ten o'clock at night), when they said they wanted to introduce us to
somebody. You see, now that I had Bennett who could speak a little
Italian, I was much better off than I had been as to knowing what was
going on. This chap was introduced to us as an Italian Communist, the
big Communist of that area. Right away he told us that he could get
us into Rome; not only get us to Rome, but see that we were taken care
of when we got there. That was the important thing. We had heard—
or Bennett had heard—a lot of this talk, and I had heard a lot of it, so
our atttitude was not at all one of being grateful; it was one of extreme
skepticism. But we said it sounded like a good idea: "If you can produce
the goods within five days, a thousand lire apiece and a suit of clothes,
we will go into Rome with you, but if not, we are going to push on, as
we are going through the line at Sulmona. We will wait five days."

The thing that decided me definitely on that course of action was the
fact that Bennett's shoes were in such poor shape that he really was not
able to travel very well. We began to realize how vital your feet are as
soon as we got going; if you haven't shoes on, you just can't move. So we
waited and at the end of five days our Communist was back; he was not
only back, but he had a thousand lire for each of us, and a civilian suit
of clothes for each of us. The prospect of getting to Rome began to
look a little more rosy.

The night of the fifth day this Communist took us into the nearby
town of Rignano, about thirty miles from Rome. Inside was a compatriot who lived there. He was the one that was going to get us into
Rome along with his wife. So that night we had to go to bed fairly
early, because going into Rome meant that you left on the four o'clock
interurban. The reason the interurban had to run so early was that

anything that ran in daylight was machine-gunned; no one dared to travel to Rome in daylight. That was a good sign right there; it meant that everyone on the train would be sleepy and cross and minding his own business.

They bought the tickets that morning, and that was exciting. They wouldn't let me wear my glasses because that was a give-away. Actually I was in the section now where people did wear glasses, but I didn't know that; so I took them off, and that made me feel uneasy. I wasn't quite so sure without my glasses. We went through the streets of this town and down to the station to buy the tickets. The train was right on the button. Of course, it has to be, for if it wasn't on time and the daylight caught it, it would just have the devil knocked out of it.

We got on the train, sat down in our seats, the conductor came along and he asked one man for his identification papers, but he didn't ask us, thank goodness, and we rolled into Rome. Under her arm, the woman was carrying my uniform, dirty as it could be, of course, wrapped up in a piece of newspaper. We got to the station and, much to my satisfaction, there was no check-up there. But again I almost kicked myself through the roof of the car. I had been given the stub of my ticket; I wasn't going to lose that stub, for it was necessary to present it at the other end; and so I put it in my pocket. I was all ready to go through the gate in Rome, when I reached for the ticket and it was gone. You can imagine my feelings; how was I going to get out of the gates? I was going to be caught just due to sheer, unadulterated carelessness; you can realize how frantically I was searching. Finally I found it at the last second.

8

THERE WE WERE IN ROME, practically right in the heart of Rome. It was quite a feeling, and of course I still had on my big military boots; but that didn't mean much either because anybody that had shoes at all, no matter what they looked like, would wear them. I saw a very charming young lady walking along the street in dead summer in a pair of ski boots. So you see what the shoe leather situation in Italy is.

From there we were taken to a fine big apartment house. The keeper of the apartment house, the keeper of the door, really rules the Roman apartment house because he knows everything, sees everybody that goes in and comes out of his apartment. In the basement was kind of a clearing house for prisoners coming into Rome. He was to be our guide.

From there I was cleared to a family. I had to leave Bennett because two men being billeted on one family was hard on them with the food situation what it was. I had made arrangements to receive a certain stipend every month to pay for my board and room.

I was taken to an Italian family and oh, were they frightened! They wanted me to stay right in my room every minute. Of course it wasn't a bad idea but it was hard on me. I would pace up and down the room, and I said to myself, "Well, you can't fritter your time away and you'll learn Italian at last." My host had an English and Italian dictionary and I was plowing away and getting absolutely nowhere. I had been there only three days when along came Lt. Simpson.

Lt. Simpson had been in the artillery of the British Army and had been taken at Tobruk. He had been a prisoner in a prison camp at Sulmona for a year and a half. In September, 1943, the prison camp was thrown open and Simpson and some of his cohorts had moved into the nearby town of Sulmona. They lived very well until they had to leave; maybe someone had talked too much, but they had to leave Sulmona and had settled in Rome. They had a very snappy little officers' organization by this time. This organization was primarily Simpson and a chap named Major Fen Harvey (I don't know how much he did); but Simpson was distributing money to men not only inside Rome but those on the fringes outside.

Simpson was the leader, father confessor, and business agent for his group of men. They were all British with the exception of one escaped aviator and myself. In America there is a commonly accepted idea that the Germans shoot a recaptured escaped prisoner. That is not so, at least as far as the British and the Americans go. I think the Germans might shoot an escaped Russian or Pole when they recapture him, but they treat the escaped British and Americans practically the same as we treat the escaped German prisoner in this country.

Captain Wilson drifted into our group; he was a British officer who had escaped for the third time. When the hand bills came out announcing that the Germans were offering a 60,000 lire reward for Captain Wilson a printer knew exactly where Captain Wilson could be found. Being a typical Italian business man, the printer felt that he could not overlook such an opportunity. So he began to toy with the idea of turning Wilson in. Also with a typical Italian peculiarity, he could not simply turn Captain Wilson in secretly; he must salve his conscience by asking several of his friends if they did not think he should do it. I suppose they advised him to do it but one of them proceeded to warn Lt. Simpson. Therefore, when the SS Troopers called at the apartment where Wilson had been staying Wilson had been gone for two hours.

This story illustrates business ethics in Rome. Do not do a dirty trick unless several of your friends tell you it is all right.

Americans pride themselves on their gift for organization; but no one could have done a finer job of organizing something out of nothing than was done by Lt. Simpson. He arrived in Rome six or seven months before I got there, without friends or connections—his only acquaintance, the underground who brought him in—and by the time I arrived there Rome was his oyster. If you wanted a tailor you asked Lt. Simpson; if it was a bootmaker you needed, Lt. Simpson would produce him; change in billets, cigarettes, wine—Lt. Simpson was your man. He wished no praise; he did not even seem to care for appreciation of his work. If it interfered with his play—he loved to play—it was simply too bad, a bore. He felt that it was his duty as an officer and gentleman to do the work.

As long as England has men like Lt. Simpson scattered everywhere in the world she is going to make a quick recovery.

I had the real names of Chicken and Dinger in my pocket along with their serial numbers, and since this chap was British I pulled these names out and told him they were British and told him to try and get these names sent home as mine was to be, and gave him mine to be sent again. That warmed his heart and he had two thousand more lire for me. The pay per month was three thousand lire and I had received one thousand in the country and he had two thousand more there in the city. Simpson said, "I've a Major that is supposed to be coming in from the country tomorrow; I've a good billet for him, but if he is not here tomorrow and since you are not so happy here and I've some enlisted men I want to put in the billet, I'll come around and get you and leave the enlisted men here and take you to this other billet."

Next morning there he was, very snappily dressed, briefcase under his arm, just a picture of the Roman business man. I was, at the moment he arrived, about to dive into a bowl of delicious macaroni, homemade of course, with nice meat sauce over it. I had finally worked this family into giving me a decent portion, for they had been very skimpy at first, and I hadn't complained but just looked rather hurt and injured over the meager fare. Since I was pulling out I had to leave that lunch for the chap that was coming in and as I had just sat down, I had to get up. Simpson saw my embarrassment over missing the meal. He said, "Come along with me and we'll eat at the Casino della Rosa.'' Here I was with my army boots and an ill-fitting prisoner civilian suit, and he was going to take me to the Casino della Rosa.

The Casino della Rosa is in the fine park called Umberto, right on the edge near the section of the old Roman wall, a lovely place. Everybody would walk in; Simpson was talking in English to me, of course not loudly or shouting. We walked up to the bar and Simpson talked first in Italian to the bartender and then in English. The bartender spoke English—perfect English; in fact, he had lived in New York for a long time, and kicked himself for ever going back to Italy. We would buy a drink and he would buy a drink. We bought some cigarettes. The bartender had saved cigarettes for Simpson, at a heavy price. Then we went into the dining room. We ordered a meal and only five tables away sat two German officers, with close cropped hair, trying to look as fierce as they could. I sat there looking right at them. We had a good meal, got up and left with no trouble at all. Then I was taken on to my new billet.

This billet was with a woman of about thirty-seven or eight years; her husband was a Major in the Italian army and at that time he was a— well, I don't know what you would call him; he wasn't a prisoner because of the armistice, but he was being held in a British concentration camp in Bombay, India. Her thought was that if she could befriend an American, her husband's repatriation might be speeded up; that was the basis on which she had been sold on taking me in. She was living with her aged mother, about eighty, an Englishwoman who had forgotten her English and who could speak to me only in Italian.

Our fare was very meager but it was quite a step-up in the world from where I had been. It was evidently the home of cultured people, with a few English books around; very well decorated with nice-looking things and a nice place to be. Then a terrible thing happened to me. I hadn't been there very long when Simpson came along to get me and take me over to another family. There I met a lot of Britishers, and they were all dressed up to the minute. There was Gerry and Cecil, and Major Fen Harvey and Bill Simpson and Pat Wilson, an American from the Detroit Bank who had been in the R.A.F. and decided to stay and become a British citizen, and a boy called Duke (from New Orleans), who had been in on the bombing of Rome and was shot down. Some of them were very snappy, and here I was in my old prisoner's suit. So, right away, Mrs. L, who was a French woman, had to get me tailored and fixed up, and right away I must buy a good-looking suit from a friend of theirs; so I did—eight thousand lire—just chicken feed.

I bought the suit and the next day was going out to lunch and wanted to look snappy; I had the underwear on I had been wearing for two months. I took it off and washed it with cold water, and hung it up to dry. I had no underwear to put on so I put on my shirt and my new stuff and off we went to the Casino della Rosa, where I was taking Mrs. L out to lunch. As soon as I got home I was cold and I rushed right in to get that underwear. All the cold water had done was to drive the lice up to the surface. I hadn't known I was lousy but there they were, and boy! I was really lousy! I got it on and then put my good suit back on, which was the tragedy of the thing; and then I felt something on the back of my neck and reached around and here he was, just as big as life, just a little bit better than an eighth of an inch long. Well, I peeled that suit off in nothing flat because I didn't want to contaminate my brand new suit. There I was—and this lovely Italian woman; how was I going to explain to her that I was lousy and how was I going to explain without getting thrown out?

So, I asked her to call Lt. Simpson and get him over here right away. She did speak a little English. He came over and I explained my dilemma and he gave me a lot of powder; so for the next three days I sat around the room powdering myself and my bed and my clothes and everything in sight, and I did kill them all, finally.

9

THE JERRIES SAID that Rome was an open city, but actually they were moving stuff through all the time. The apartment house that I was in was right on the Via Flaminia, the main north-south road through Rome, and all the Jerries were marching up and down that road at night, moving troops in and moving empty trucks out. I could hear them coming by. I heard a lot of horse-drawn stuff come by. They had a lot of horse-drawn equipment down there.

After about ten days the woman with whom I was staying began to get a little nervous; this was her first prisoner and although I was standing in real well, she wanted me to go somewhere else. Another billet was found for me with a younger woman and her mother. Theirs was a very fine apartment, which they owned. The apartment was built by a building association and they purchased their apartment. It was located on a street called Arezzo, same name as the town I had come down from. It was really a fine apartment, with many English books, and these people spoke four or five languages, including English. They had lost all their money. She had been very wealthy in her own right and had married a nice chap and he had died. She had turned all her affairs over to a lawyer; he had absolutely fleeced her; she had got the law on him and put him in prison and a year later he was out, but with all the money, of course.

So, except for this apartment, she had nothing, and she and her daughter were giving lessons to earn money; you can imagine, all white-collar stuff, on the old Roman scale of pay—you know, fifteen or twenty lire for a day's work and inflation had already begun. So these people were just barely getting along. I stayed there for fourteen days and it was awfully hard in the little apartment. I consumed every English book in it and was becoming more and more restless and finally they agreed to let me out twice a week, but always I had to pass the doorman who knew all, saw all, and heard all in Rome.

I had been going out very quietly and walking in the very beautiful park. Not only would I walk in the park, but by this time I began to know the region and feel confident, in an area of about two or three square miles. I walked around fairly freely, feeling that if I did have to run or hide or dodge somewhere I would know where to go within my own little area. I didn't go out of that area but, fortunately, it included the fine park, the Casino della Rosa, and also ran on down, going to the west to the Tiber River, along the Tiber just where the bridge is, with the Palace of Justice at the other end. On my side of the Tiber, that is to say on the east bank, was the Orco, a fine eating place, which all the escaped prisoners patronized. I had all those things to move about in; there were the two of the finest eating places in Rome and a lot of good shops, and not only that, but it was one of the better districts of Rome and not too many people in it—fine wide streets, tree-covered, and very pleasant. Of course this moving around as I did cost a great deal of money.

But I had two sources of money; one was the stipend that I received every month for room and board, and the other was chits that I was cashing. Now a chit is simply a check written out against your bank—in other words, a promise to pay—and I was writing my checks out against the Wabeek State Bank, Detroit, where Dad and I had a joint bank account. My primary reason was to get money, but I began to think it over a little bit after the first check and said, "There is no better way to inform the family every month that you are all right." I was convinced that the family already knew that I was all right because I had twice been told that my name had been sent home. This was a way of repeating that I was all right. Although I am running ahead of the story, I cashed in Rome four hundred dollars worth of checks, all drawn on the Wabeek State Bank, about a hundred dollars a month. The checks were dated and marked "Rome." Feeling that a speculator, as this chap was, had to have a rapid turnover, I was convinced that everyone at home knew I was all right, in Rome, and well. Naturally, if I cashed all those checks I must be living a pretty high life.*

One evening I took a lady out to dinner at the Casino della Rosa. She called my attention to four men sitting at the next table, not over eight feet away. She said, "Those are the head of the Gestapo in Rome and his three assistants." I got the impression that the chief Jerry was looking at me rather often and I began to think of taking off. I was especially interested when he got up and left the table to telephone. I called the waiter and asked him to check on him. The waiter came back in a few minutes and said, "Routine call." A rather amusing picture— the waiter leaning over the shoulder of the chief of the Gestapo, listening to his telephone call and the waiter and I conferring about the matter in English, with the three assistants only eight feet away.

Even more amusing is the fact that all four of them hung their Lügers in the check room with their hats; same theory as the old western practice of checking the revolvers with the bar-keeper. There was no one in the check room and I had an overpowering desire to take the Lüger of the chief of the Gestapo as a souvenir, but finally conquered this desire when I realized that the Jerries would simply wreck the Casino della Rosa if this happened.

Every waiter and every bartender in the better places in Rome knew that we were escaped prisoners. They simply did not betray us because of professional pride. It is true that our little group of ten men, with the help of a few German officers, practically kept the Casino della Rosa alive, so that may have been a factor. We would pay 500 lire for a single dinner.

For one reason and another, perhaps primarily because my hosts were growing, as the British would say, "windy," which is to say frightened, I had to move again. I was a little bit tired of having to move,

---

*[None of these checks ever reached the bank.]

and I would try hard to make myself part of the family. I had stayed for one day at the French Seminary. The French Seminary is located right back of the old Pantheon. That was the way I could always find it. The bill of fare hadn't been very good there but it was enough to live on and the room was satisfactory. It was a big building, and you could walk around in it. And not only that, but I had had some experiences that had sobered me up a little. I will tell you some of them.

The British I met had been in Rome a long time and, as the British say, were growing browned off; that is to say, they were growing disgusted that the Allies had not arrived. They all had plenty of money; they had all found people to cash personal checks, in addition to what they were receiving as a stipend every month. They were dressed right up to the minute, and were eating at all the good cafes; and, of course, since they had been in Rome much longer, their area was much larger than mine. In fact, the whole city was their area—not only the whole city, but many of the beautiful girls in that city.

And the snappiest dressed fellow and the best-looking fellow and a really good egg was a chap named Gerry, an R.A.F. captain who had been shot down in Africa. Gerry had hooked onto a very nice looking Countess. She had a little money in her own right, and was a very snappy dresser. Gerry was the very height of fashion, with a black Homburg hat, a dark-striped, tailored suit, what looked like an Arrow collar on his shirt, nice cravat, good-looking shoes made in Rome—if you had the money you could get anything—and a dark coat with satin lapels. He was taking this young lady out one day on the tram, going somewhere. On this tram were two Fascist thugs, special police, rough-looking fellows. They generally went around dressed in leather short coats, riding-breeches, and boots, carrying a machine pistol or a rifle, or an ordinary automatic pistol, and were pretty tough fellows. They saw this fellow all spicked up and they saw this girl wearing furs, very lovely, and all dressed up, and they think, "We will embarrass this fellow. We may be able to shake him down for some money, cause him some trouble."

They begin to look at him, look him up and down and figure him out a little bit, and he sees that. So the first time the tram stops, he just swings on off, and they swing off too. He walks a little faster along the street, and they walk a little faster. He turns a corner and they turn the same corner. So he sees just what the game is, and where he made his error; he should have just taken off on the run once he got a little distance. He looks in the store windows to see if he is really being followed. He is. They walk up and say, *"Documenti!"*, which means that he is to produce his documents. He has some forged documents, not very good ones. They look at them. They make him talk a bit and they know right away that they have something. So they say, "Well, all right, we are going to take you down to the station." They start to lead him off. One of them has a machine pistol; that is just what it means, you see, a full automatic pistol, a very nice weapon, a German weapon, with a very high rate of fire, holding about a thirty- or fifty-round magazine. That was the dangerous weapon. The other man is armed with a semi-automatic pistol. You must pull the trigger every time. The machine one, the Americans call it a burp-gun; you just hold it down; there is just a b-rr-rrr-pp. It's gone, you see; the whole magazine.

So he suddenly turns and knocks the fellow with the machine pistol end over end. He is about six feet one. He just knocks him flatter than a pancake and takes off, counting on the fact that the man with the pistol, who is nervous, can't hit very much. He's shooting at Gerry just ahead of him all the time, dodging and twisting with the other fellow after him, with his compatriot up off the pavement by that time too, both mad as hornets. Of course, they would have killed him in a second if they had caught him.

I was an innocent participant in the affair; innocent because I was up in the L apartment having a quiet cup of tea and minding my own business when we hear this shooting. I just think it's a car backfiring, but Adrian, who has been through the mill on those things, says, "Look out of the window," and I do. Gerry at that point had just rounded the corner of our building, like a rabbit looking for a hole, and the Fascist is running after him, shooting at every jump. I don't know what he is shooting at; I can't see Gerry. Well, as soon as Gerry gets around the corner, he darts into our building, you see! Three seconds later, there is a frantic ringing of the doorbell, and there is Gerry, white as a sheet, and Mrs. L hands him the keys and sends him on up, on to the roof, to hide. Of course the obvious conclusion to draw from that is that soon the Fascists will be in the building. They have gathered in a little knot on the corner, walking up and down the street, trying to figure where the chap had gone. She has got to get me out fast before they get in, so she hands me my hat and coat and says, "O.K., get going!"

I take the elevator down and walk out; they are standing in a knot on one of the street corners. If I walk away, they will probably yell for me to come to them, and question me; but if I walk right on up to them they probably won't say anything. So instead of walking away from the group, I walk right on up to these Italians; and by that time a crowd has gathered. Italians are terrible in crowds and silly, because if a German has been killed, let's say, and a crowd gathers, pretty soon the Jerries come up, pull everybody in, and it doesn't matter who those people are, if they are Italians, they just shoot them all.

Why crowds gather is a mystery; but they had gathered, which helped me, of course, because I just walked on right through the crowd and was gone. Then they began to wise up finally after all the chatter, and they came to look in our building—this apartment. Fortunately, for Gerry and the L's, the L's owned a basement apartment, and in that a *carabiniere* was staying. (*Carabinieri* is just another name for the municipal policemen of Rome, who were pretty good eggs.) He was hard up, living on a meager salary, and they let him live down there. He knew what the score was, he had seen Gerry come in; when these fellows come in, there he stood right in the hall. They asked him, "Have you seen an escaped prisoner come in?" He said, "No, no, but where is he? Give me a gun and I'll help you look for him." Of course that indicated to them that no one had come and they went away.

One afternoon four of us had met at L's for tea. We are sitting visiting when the door bell rings. Mrs. L answers and in march three SS troopers. They have come to pick up the fourteen year old L boy. His name is on the list of pupils of a Communist professor whom they have recently picked up. He is at home, so they order him to prepare to leave with them and they also order Mr. L to go along with them. There *we* are, four strange men, and they do not say a word to us.

They take the L's to headquarters and report that there were four strange men in the apartment. They are immediately ordered to come back and pick us up. We, naturally, are not there when they get back. Mrs. L explains that she does not know our names, that we had simply dropped in, and she gets away with some kind of a cock-and-bull story. I think this story illustrates the reason the Germans were not able really to control Rome very effectually.

The Fascists and the Germans decided to have a big May Day parade in Rome. Things went off according to schedule and fortunately I did not choose this day to go out and look around. With typical Italian lack of common sense, the Communists decided to throw some bombs into the parade and kill some Jerries. They did kill thirty-two Jerry soldiers riding in trucks.

The Germans immediately threw a cordon of troops around that whole section of town and picked up the first 320 Italian men they could get their hands on. Many of these were prominent lawyers, doctors, and merchants. They took the whole bunch out to a cave outside of Rome and machine-gunned them in the cave and then blew the mouth of the cave shut with dynamite.

As many of these were the most respected citizens of Rome this caused great sorrow. I was living at the A's at this time and the two women walked up and down the apartment wringing their hands. I could understand their sorrow the first day and the second day and even the third day; but when they kept up their wailing for a week it began to get on my nerves. I told them that if such a thing happened in our country the women would begin to plan vengeance instead of just continuing to cry and agonize.

The Italian people are very volatile. In my first days in Rome, out somewhere at tea I would meet a young Italian anti-Fascist army officer. He would talk freely about what he was doing in the way of anti-Fascist activities. The next week I would hear he had been picked up and shot. This never seemed to give the Italians pause and make them realize they were in a game of life and death. The whole thing seemed like a glorified opera to them in which they were anxious to play their parts in conversation.

10

I SAW INFLATION in Rome. It is really worse than war in the way it disorganizes a community. One could obtain anything in a black market but the prices in Italian money were scandalous; and this high black market naturally disorganizes the regular economy.

As a hedge, I sent L out in the black market to buy a considerable quantity of flour and olive oil. His first purchase was only two barrels of flour and a keg of olive oil. Taking care of this got to be such a chore that I decided not to buy any more. I had made great plans to sell it as soon as our troops came into Rome and make a tidy profit, but when our troops did come I forgot all about my good resolutions and gave the supplies to my friends the Irish priests.

Then we had another thing happen that began to make me want to look for a new billet. In April, as a kind of an Easter celebration, we all went to the apartment of Madame M, a Maltese woman who was taking care of five prisoners, two Americans and three British—three British also off the submarine *Saracen*. There we are at her apartment. She has fixed up quite a whirl, tea and cake and everything she can get hold of. All of us in there, all of the officers and a bunch of enlisted men, all that can get there, singing and raising hell. At that point Simpson walks in, at three o'clock in the afternoon, and tells us that twenty-five enlisted men whom he knew, have just been picked up! Someone has spilled the beans. Of course we take off out of there.

After having had these two experiences, seeing that the escaped British had forgotten that they were in an Italian German-patrolled town, all I wanted was a quiet place; just a real quiet home, see? I remembered the French Seminary. The reason the seminary was open was that ever since the days of Napoleon, whenever France is threatened, everybody is called up in the draft—that includes everybody. There is no such thing as a conscientious objector, no such thing as a man of God, or anything. Everybody, and that includes the priests, grabs a rifle and goes off and starts shooting. All these young fellows being trained in the seminary and all of the priests already ordained who were young enough went home.

When Italy stabbed France in the back and naturally sent soldiers around to close the seminary, in the discussion Father Monier, the Father Superior, casually said, "This is a Papal seminary." The Italian soldiers confused that, which is simply a charter, with extra-territorial rights. Then they went off and left it because there was nobody in it anyhow. That was a pretty good place to be, then, and that is why it was operating. To make this establishment run as a business venture—here was a big building; you had to keep it up—Father Monier had taken in various people that he had okayed. First, there was a lot of Italian Jews who were trying to hole up until the storm was over. He had also taken in some Italian priests that had been bombed out of Frascati, and he had five young Frenchmen who had come down from France to escape the labor draft.

I had been there only a day, on my return, when a French flight-lieutenant came in who had been shot down in Africa, from the same prison camp the Britishers had been in at Solum. He had been the purveyor of food, had been allowed to go outside the camp, and had simply taken off on one of his purveying trips; had come to Rome, been very ill with pneumonia, had just moved out of the hospital there in Rome before the Jerries raided it, recovered a little bit, and now moved into the French Seminary. In all there were, I should say, fifty Italian Jews, myself, and the French lieutenant, and five of these young French fellows in age ranging around from about nineteen to about twenty-two. That was our little group in the seminary.

In addition to the group I have just described, we had there two Irish priests who gave me a lot of pleasure while I was at the Seminary. Unfortunately for these poor chaps, their Order in Ireland was the same Order as the one Father Monier presided over; so instead of being able to go to the jolly Irish seminary, which was running full blast in Rome, with good times and plenty of food and jolly good fellows, they had to come to this straight-laced, pinchpenny French seminary. They were pretty good scouts, and every day I had tea with them. I was able to have tea because I had accumulated several checks that I hadn't cashed and decided to go to the black market myself to protect myself from the black market, because nobody could cenceivably live on any ration that you could get under the rationing system.

I had purchased several kilos of flour, a few litres of olive oil, a few kilos of sugar and as much tea as I could get hold of; in other words, all the staples I could. I was pretty well set, and when I moved into the Seminary I moved all these things with me. The only place to put them was down in Father O'Brien's room. I had them all stacked down there in Father O'Brien's closet, all this food. Every so often the priests would—really this was a great secret—they would slip a little flour and a little sugar and a little olive oil out and would have some of their good friends in the other seminaries make them up some cookies and crackers and we would have a little something for tea; high tea we would have twice a week from these things that were made up for us.

I would suggest that we invite some of the French priests and they would say, "Oh, don't do that; don't do that; we can't stand them. Don't have them in here. They just pinch us down to the last threadbare item, the last threadbare item." Now these poor chaps had taken the three most stringent vows of the Catholic Church; that is, they had taken the vow of celibacy, the vow of poverty, and I suppose it is the vow of humiliation, or something, and they were really threadbare, not a cent to their names. The good Father Superior picked up all the ration cards for tobacco, which was the only thing you could get in very small quantities. At first it was forty cigarettes a week; then it dropped down to thirty, and later to twenty. The priests couldn't even get those. They didn't really want the tobacco, but they wanted to be able to give it to me. So the idea of giving anything to these French just cut them to the quick; and when I told them that I was paying a little bit above the average rate, they just wrung their hands in horror that this was being done.

Of course, it sounded like a fortune to them. Actually, I was not paying very much considering the inflation that was taking place in Rome. That is, I had been paying a hundred lire a day. When I went to this seminary, I wanted to stay permanently. I knew that Father Monier was a good business man, and I wanted to make it worth his while, so I gave him 150 lire a day. The Irish priests thought that was just fantastic. Translated into eggs, of which they had none, at fourteen lire an egg, they began to figure all the eggs they could buy for 150 lire a day.

I had a lot of long talks with these fellows about England and Ireland and the Irish question, and if there was anybody they hated, it was the English. They were priests, it was true, of the Catholic Church; but when it came to England, that was another matter—another matter entirely! I tried to argue a little on the English side, but I couldn't get very far. The only people they disliked worse than the English were the French! These poor chaps had been in Italy for five years. They had arrived without being able to speak French, and it had taken them a year to learn. All the lessons were conducted in Latin, but the ordinary conversation around the Seminary was in French. They had had to learn French in addition to their Latin, and they had also had to pick up Italian. I would have have expected that these two guys would have had some quarrels, but, you know, being driven so closely together by the outside pressure of the world, and the Seminary in particular, which was their world, had only solidified their good Irish friendship. One was Father O'Brien and the other was Father O'Connor. I don't suppose you can get any better Irish names than that and they really looked Irish. They were literal believers in the Bible, absolutely to the letter. I would shock them with heresies, but they enjoyed it; it was the first time they had ever been shocked, apparently.

My friends, the Irish priests, were constantly bewailing their sad fate. They were marooned in Rome without any money and without any hope of obtaining any. They had at last obtained their doctor's degrees and were ready to go back to Ireland; but how were they going to get there? Being held in Rome so long, they had spent the money they originally had to take them home. They did not know whether their Order in Ireland would send them any. I, therefore, told them I would loan them nine thousand lire to get back to Ireland. They almost fainted. They had been in Rome when one could get the finest dinner at the Casino della Rosa that anyone would ask for, with a bottle of good wine, for fifteen lire; and even when I was in Rome a workman was receiving five or six lire a day in wages and white-collar workers were receiving fifteen lire a day; so it really looked like a fortune to them. This good deed cost me $60. It was worth it to me to feel for a moment like an American millionaire; and the strange thing is that some day I will receive a check in payment of the debt from the good fathers.

I should say a word about Father Flaherty. He was the good angel of all escaped prisoners until things got too hot for him and he had to retire into the Vatican. I cannot give you the details, but this worthy man risked his life for all of us day after day, and was one of the very few people that I met in Rome who I felt was aiding the escaped prisoner for humanitarian reasons. Almost everyone else was doing it for selfish personal reasons. Most of them made very clear to you that they expected the Allies to do a lot for them as soon as Rome was occupied— give them jobs, I mean, or some other thing that they wanted.

The French lieutenant was quite a fellow too. We had a lot of games of chess, since there was nothing else to do. We played fifty-four games and I was finally the winner, being ahead three games out of fifty-four, and triumphant. We were so tired of chess at the end of that session that we couldn't look a chessboard in the face any more. He was an Air Corps man, but for an Air Corps man he was a darn good infantry officer.

He got the French boys together, and we rigged out a regular watch that we put on night and day. We had a regular guard rotated at the main doors, and had a hiding place so if the Fascists or the SS did come to the Seminary for a routine search, we would be able to hide. We had a very dandy place. I told you that there were fifty Italian Jews living up above us on the third floor. They had a hiding place, but would they put out a guard? Absolutely not. We never could get them to put out a guard or help us a bit until the last critical days, when it was obvious that it was terribly critical; then they did come and help us guard. On the other hand, you have got to smile because earlier the

British had been in the seminary and did raise the devil; parties all night long, drink gallons of *vino*—imagine this going on in a seminary! They would have young women come and meet them down in the parlor; they just had everything in a turmoil! And there was a scare during those days when the Jews watched frantically and the British wouldn't watch at all. So you see things were pretty well mixed up.

And oh yes, I forgot to mention Edmund the Pole. Edmund was just a piggy little fellow with little shifty eyes. We all distrusted Edmund. His story was that he had come out of Poland and killed many Germans on the way. Kind of an ingratiating little fellow that irritated you with his ingratiation. The kind of fellow you felt had really no good will. Well, it proved that we were right. He forgets the hardships of the German labor battalions where he really came from. He forgets how much better off he is. He just sees he hasn't got quite as much money as the rest of us have, so, to rectify that situation he steals two thousand lire from the Father Superior, the very hand that is feeding him, and one of the Italian Jews sees this and reports. So we get hold of Edmund, and lo and behold! he has about fifteen hundred lire on him— having spent the other five hundred. He denies it all, but he doesn't want to see the Italian Jew who saw him; he doesn't want to be faced with the evidence.

We don't know what to do with him because a guy who will steal two thousand lire will sell everybody out for fifty or sixty thousand. This discovery is made about eight o'clock at night, that is, after the curfew, which was seven-thirty at that time. We know he can't get anywhere that night, so we decide that one of us had better get up in the morning, so he just doesn't slip out in the morning. I do get up about five-thirty. I heard Edmund splashing around in there getting washed at about six o'clock, which is much earlier than any of us ever got up. (Our theory was, "Stay up late at night and sleep as late as you can; that kills the day faster.") There is Edmund. Pretty soon his door opens. He has a package under his arm, all ready to leave. First I put him right back in the room. Then one of the Polish Fathers—there was a Polish Father there too— goes in to see him and comes out and tells us he is writing a letter. We go in and there is the letter addressed to the German police, naming fifty Italian Jews and one American and six Frenchmen, one of whom is a flight officer. That was pretty doggone grave—exposing the whole seminary.

So I came about as close to premeditated murder as I ever have in my life. I didn't know what we should do with this chap. Here we had him locked in his room, you see; the windows screwed shut and guard on the door—that made another guard we had to put out, but by this time we did have the Jews cooperating. The Edmund episode got them pretty well worried; that started them cooperating, you see. Well, I decided how I was going to kill this guy because we couldn't have him around. I finally decided. I looked all around and found there was a basement, not a good place to hide, but a basement with a dirt floor. I decided I would just strangle him. Then the question came whether I would make him dig the grave or go to all the work of digging it myself. And finally I decided—I didn't know how I was going to do it—but Edmund would have to dig it because I would be damned if I would dig a hole of that size in that cellar. That was really the important point. As far as Edmund's death was concerned, in the mental discussion over the hole, Edmund's fate was entirely lost in the shuffle, you see. Edmund was only eighteen. If he had been any older I wouldn't have waited. My theory was that we would tell nobody. I would tell only the French lieutenant, and we would finish him off; he would just be gone from the Seminary the next day. We would say he had left.

Then the French lieutenant pulled a phony drill on us. It was a good drill. We thought it was real, but it wasn't, the test really being, would Edmund come along without trouble? Edmund came without any trouble. If Edmund had put up any resistance, of course, it would have been impossible to let him live, but he saved himself right there. We later pulled another drill; he came along again. I decided, and the French lieutenant concurred, that due to his extreme youth, and the fact that he was taking part in these drills, we would let him survive. It was very interesting.

11

THERE WAS A FINE PLACE to walk, a nice big roof we could walk around in the evening, and you could hear the guns down at the beachhead, and on a heavy night see the reflections of flashes in the sky. We had a good radio; we were getting all the dope. I was getting awfully fed up, and the climax came when Gerry told me I might get out north if I would go up towards Ancona, and gave me the name of the town, but wouldn't tell me whom to see because Fen Harvey had told him not to tell anybody! The British were keeping that as kind of an escape door, you see. I wasn't supposed to know. Why should I know? After all, why not?

It would spoil it—too many people knowing. But I had known enough so that once I had got to that town I wouldn't have any trouble finding out the rest.

Now I was just about ready to take off; of course I was worried if I took off north and the line did come ahead there, for I would be back of the line again. The radio gave the dope again. That was May 11; the drive was starting. I said I'd wait a little while, and with every day's news you could feel the momentum of this drive; and I knew what we had at Anzio, and the Germans hadn't been able to push us out of there, with all the stuff they had thrown in. Once the thing had started I was convinced it was coming; and every radio report added to that. I got tired of all this excitement on the radio. The French were always there ahead of me anyhow with their French program. I didn't pay much attention. Every day the French would come and tell us everything was going fine, so I didn't even listen to the radio.

Of course we put on a better and better guard as things got tighter and tighter. It was pretty dangerous to move outside anywhere because as the days of the city were numbered, the Fascists under Jerry control were trying to drain the city of labor. They would just block off a long street, pick up every man in the street, make him produce his papers and German work document, and if he couldn't off he would go to work. They would stop a tram and do the same thing. So I went out, I suppose between the time when I got to the seminary about April or a little bit later, and June 5, when our men arrived, not over two times. One time was to buy a watch. I put six thousand lire down and told the owner I would pay him by June 5, thinking that I could sell my suit—my good suit—because I didn't need it in the Seminary. Then L fell down on me. He couldn't sell the suit. And there I was stuck. I wanted to sell the suit and pay the rest of the money on the watch because I figured, with this terrible inflation going on and my six thousand lire deposit, if I could sell my suit and make a lot of money I would clear my watch and not spend a thing. But I got worried about the watch and nothing happened, so I had to go and clean up the deal. That was one time I went out.

Well, we kept watching and waiting and the gunfire kept getting closer and closer—but I must stop a second and go back. I told you how the streets were shut off and trams searched. Just after I had moved into the Seminary, Simpson was apprehended. What happened was this.

At one of the parties he had met a German Jewess and she had introduced him to some Fascists who, he thought, were playing both games. So he decided to stay at their house, on the theory that in the wolf's den was a good place to hide. His theory was that they were ready to jump either way, and that that would be a good place to stay.

Along with him he took Duke. Duke, as you recall, was the American Air Force bomber pilot from New Orleans, and Duke was quite a drinker. Women were coming back and forth up to his apartment. They hadn't been there two days when the SS men walked in and picked 'em up. You can imagine what a furor that threw into our little group, to have our leader, who was distributing all the money and doing all the work, picked up suddenly. Everybody else became mighty doggone quiet after that and boy! was I saying "Hallelujah!" that I was in the French Seminary where I could stay put and not have to move. These other fellows were moving every night from one place to the other to be safe. That really calmed all the high life down. The story was that they thought the Fascists had done this thing, but there was another story that Madame L told which sounds pretty good. These women kept coming up and she told me that one night Duke was kind of drunk and he kicks one girl out of bed and told her off. She could easily have been the one who did it because her charms were spurned. Anyway, they were gone and first they were taken to Via Tasso; and Via Tasso had a pretty deadly name. The Pope had been able to do practically nothing about it. If an Italian got into Via Tasso the SS just beat him up unmercifully, and that is where these enlisted men that I mentioned, who had been picked up around Easter, had been sent. One of the Italians working with the gang, and knowing the whole story, had been caught and taken there; they had really given him a good going over, and he told everything and agreed to work for them and round these fellows up. I can understand his caving in under the beating, because for him it was life or death and for the prisoners it was simply back to a prison camp. But to flip-flop over and to be actively working for them—and from then on he was on the Fascist side, engaged in rounding up all the prisoners he could find—was a little too much.

John Furman took over. John was a very fine chap but not the Italian linguist that Simpson had been. John had quite an interesting experience. He was picked up on a tram; the tram was stopped, blocked off at both ends, and everybody taken off and into a little courtyard to have their papers looked at. All those who couldn't produce satisfactory documents were sent down to police headquarters and there allocated to a labor gang. Among all these Italians, John, of course, was the only Englishman, and the Italians were screaming and yelling about the indignity. There were two Italians there, two Fascists, and a couple of Germans, plus the Jerry soldiers. They were all yelling and yelling and the German would just look at their papers and say, "Over there, over there." Out of these fifteen men there were only three that were turned loose and one of them was Furman. Furman couldn't speak Italian well enough to fool anybody and if he opened his mouth they would have had him. So Furman keeps perfectly quiet and just walks over and hands them his papers and the German says, "Here's a guy that knows he is all right and keeps absolutely quiet; he's not worried." So they look at his documents and hand them back to him and out he goes. Three men out of fifteen and Furman is one of them. It shows you what being calm will do. That episode calmed the group down in addition to these other things, so for me it was just a question of waiting at the Seminary. I would hear all these stories filtering in and I would talk to them as they came around and on one of my two trips out I went to the L's apartment and got all these stories first hand.

12

ONE OCCASION THAT I DID go out was Sunday and that was when the tail end of the Jerries pulled out. I couldn't resist that. They were really beaten up, their equipment was beaten up, they were really tired, and they looked just what they were—an army retreating, but retreating in good order. And I felt for the infantry, for once these Jerry trucks started to move they didn't stop for anything; so the infantry were just slogging along on their feet and it was quite a sight to watch them. They would commandeer any car; any fool that would be riding around in a car didn't have his car very long, for the walking infantrymen would stop him and grab his car. And then along the side of the road were five Jerries sitting with their fists against their heads, a worried looking bunch of guys. Their rear tire—they had skidded around the corner—was gone and there they were with no way to move, just sitting there and looking at the car as if that was going to fix it.

The gunfire got closer and closer and pretty soon was right in the suburbs. That meant ten miles out; you could see the tracers and everything. That night I went to bed and I said, "I'm not going to run out on the streets and get shot after waiting this long to get back." But about three in the morning the Frenchmen run in and kiss me on both cheeks and hug me and say, "Put on your uniform! The Americans are here!" I wanted to say, "Well, darn it, I'll go to see 'em in the morning." But I reluctantly put on my uniform and out we sally and they take me to the Americans. It is one lone G.I. lost in the middle of the Piazza Venezia. That is the big square with a great huge Victor Emanuel monument; at the other end of it was where Mussolini made his talks. The G.I. is just standing there and what has happened is the old G.I. stuff. His unit stopped for one second and he climbed off the jeep to look around; they pulled out and there he was all alone in the middle of the square. I said, "I'll tell you what I'll do; I'll be back here for you in an hour and if they haven't picked you up by then I'll take you where I live and put you up." So at three o'clock I went back and he was gone. I went back to bed. Then bright and early the next morning I was up with my uniform on and out on the streets. It was a real sight of course. The boys were coming in and they were really tired.

The Jerries did leave a small rear guard in Rome to keep our boys from just ripping on through the town after them and there had been a pretty good scrap about four or five o'clock in the morning—Monday morning that would be. I sallied forth to see our boys and all the Romans were happy and cheering and our stuff began coming in. First, of course, the infantry and a few tanks and then later the big stuff. I couldn't find anybody that knew anything about the Rangers. I had already told the L's that I had my obligation, and that when the boys arrived I wasn't going to be around there at all. I had left a little note recommending Mr. and Mrs. L for work in the Military Administrative Embassy; so I felt that my skirts were clear.

I finally ran into some of the Special Service boys. This was a task force, half Canadians and half Americans. They were quite some chaps, particularly the top officers that I later saw. They told me that the Rangers had all been sent home except for the men that had been in only a year and under, and that those men had just been automatically put in the Special Service force; they told me where their headquarters were. I got there, and there was Brigadier General Frederick and a few of his staff. He knew all about the Rangers and took good care of me.

He took me in and talked to me and told me about his dramatic fight at the bridge—one of the bridges across the Tiber. He and the captain that had driven me down and three enlisted men had attacked the bridge. He was acting as his own first scout and they had taken fifteen Jerries over there. They had had one terrible fight and miraculously he was untouched. He was just nicked all over, though, and full of scratches, and he even had a bullet hole through the cuff of his glove. How he could get it through there I don't know, except that the glove must have been blowing out so it went right on through and never touched him.

He was just wild to get back to General Mark Clark and take him a sign saying ROMA, all full of holes. He had that sign and when he saw me he said, "You come along with me." He was going to take me as another souvenir. So, in his armored half-track we got out of the city. Within fifteen minutes, or half an hour after I left the Seminary, I was on my way out of Rome. We drove out and got to their headquarters, and they all were very glum because one of their regimental commanders had also been acting as a first scout, but he hadn't been so fortunate. A 20-mm. shell went right through the middle of his forehead. He was lying somewhere piled high with flowers that the Italians had put on him. Apparently he had been a wonderful fellow and, judging from these other men—wonderful looking men—he must have been, for they were all broken up about it. I was most impressed with them. I saw the major of their artillery and I saw their lieutenant colonel, paratroopers, and of course Brigadier General Frederick—quite an impressive array. We stayed there about an hour and I presented a bottle of champagne. I was going to give that to Father Monier when I left, but when I told the Irish that I had a bottle of champagne I was going to give to Father Monier, they said, "Don't ever do it, never do it." So I had saved that bottle and when I did pull out I went to the Seminary and got it and gave it to General Frederick. From there we transferred into his jeep and off we went.

13

I BEGAN TO SEE THE WAR. On the way out of Rome I had seen where about seven of our tanks had been knocked out along the road by well placed anti-tank guns. The tanks had just come steaming in ahead of everything else, and of course channelized on the road. The Jerry guns had just knocked 'em off. I think most of the crews were alive because the tanks didn't look burned out at all, but just stopped; there had been so many coming in that they had just bucked them aside. Then we went through the Alban battlefield; that is in the Alban Hills and all high ground; but Rome had really fallen when our troops had arrived that morning. Albano was shot up badly, and then we went through Valmontone and that was just wrecked, and I mean wrecked, the way things were in the last World War. Velletri also was flattened, and we kept on driving and driving. Truck after truck of German equipment was burning alongside of the road. Our air force just raked them and then the Germans would have to toss the vehicle to the side of the road, where they would set fire to it so it couldn't be used. Endless equipment! I saw big Tiger tanks and 88-mm. guns and other caliber guns and that made me think of the wrecked German equipment that I had seen north of Rome. The Germans themselves said that out of four trucks going from Milan to Rome only one would get through; our aircraft would get the others. There was a lot of that equipment up north where a plane could strafe it. Of course, up there they could move it at night back off the road and try to fix it, and it wasn't as bad when I came down as it was later on. I saw these towns flattened and finally we got to a place that was just a pile of rubble and the General said, "Do you recognize this?" I said, "No." He said, "This is Cisterna." Just flattened—absolutely nothing left. We went from there to the Fifth Army Headquarters.

And from there on my trip became quite routine. I was a little bit shocked at the luxury I saw at Fifth Army Headquarters and, mentally, began to criticise it when suddenly they picked up and moved to Rome, and when I arrived back in Rome they were set up in the fine Savoy Park; they looked as if they had been there for fifteen years. Everything was running smoothly, just like a big circus. I managed to get hold of some concentrated chocolate bars, and I went around to people I had been with and gave them each a package of twelve of these bars.

The British were handling the transportation of XPOW's back; so I went through the British lines until I got to Naples. There I was put in the hands of the Americans and flown to Algiers.

I almost got myself into a jam at Algiers. They wanted to know the whole story, and I wrote it for them on the typewriter. It deeply impressed the corporal who read it. I was telling him how rough the country was, and how a few men could operate up there and that if they knew what they were doing they could really cause a lot of trouble; and

I said (of course I didn't know he was going to call me on it but I was ready if anyone did) I said that I was willing to go back there with four or five men that were reliable and cause a little trouble because I knew that country. He took me over to the captain. The next day the captain called and I immediately called him back, but he had gone out to lunch. My papers were due to fly me down to Oran, so I had to leave. I ate lunch in Oran, had dinner in Casablanca, went to see "Captains Courageous" the next afternoon in Belfast, Ireland, and arrived in New York at two o'clock the next afternoon.